FOR GOLD AND BLOOD

Tana Reiff

GLOBE FEARON

HOPES *And* DREAMS

Cover photo: The Bettmann Archive, Inc.
Illustration: Tennessee Dixon

ISBN 0-8224-3679-5
Printed in the United States of America

8 9 10 11 12   06 05 04

Globe
Fearon

Pearson Learning Group

1-800-321-3106
www.pearsonlearning.com

CONTENTS

CHAPTER 1

Kwangtung Province,
China, 1851

"They call it
the Mountain of Gold!"
said Soo Lee
to his brother Ping.
"It's a place
across the ocean.
California,
I think, is the name.
A man from America
told me all about it.
People with nothing
get rich fast!
They find gold
in the hills!
And look at us.
Since the war,
we have had
no real home.
We cannot always live

in this houseboat.
Let's go
to the Mountain of Gold!"

"How can you
talk like this?"
asked Ping.
"China is
the center of the Earth.
Our family
is here.
Besides,
the country
will not let us leave."

"There are ways,"
said Soo.
"We just give
a little money
to the men
at the port.
They will see
that we get on a ship."

Ping Lee
was still not sure

he liked Soo's idea.
But the idea of gold
sounded very good.
Going to California
could help
the whole family.
He and Soo
could send gold home.
In a few years
they could come
back to China.

"Maybe you are right,"
said Ping.
"Maybe this is something
we should do.
We are
young and strong.
We are
the only ones
who can help the family."

The Lee family
was very big.
The brothers
told of their plan.

Everyone
wanted to help
raise money
for the trip.
After all,
it would help everyone.

Mother Lee
sold her special green stone.
Uncle Lo
sold his only cow.
Pretty soon,
they had put together
enough money.

Ping and Soo
took off
for Hong Kong.
Soo paid a man
to get them
on a ship.
They were packed
into the ship's hold.
They sat
on brown mats
with many other young men.

It took two months
to reach California.
A man from China
met the ship.
He gave
a pick and shovel
to each Chinese man.
They could pay
for them later.
He showed them
the way
to a gold field.
Once they got there,
someone would show them
how to find gold.

Thinking It Over

1. If you were Ping,
   would you go along
   with your brother's idea?

2. Do you think
   it was OK
   to pay to get out of China?

3. Do you believe
   in get-rich-quick ideas?
   Do you believe
   Soo and Ping
   will find gold?

CHAPTER 2

Soo and Ping
went to work
for a gold company.
Some white men
showed them
how to find gold.
Soo and Ping
learned fast.
They picked for gold
up and down the hills.
They used flat pans
to find gold
in streams.

Sure enough,
they found gold.
Sometimes
they found little pieces.
Most of the time
they found gold dust.
The white men

let them keep half
of what they found.

    The Chinese workers
were a sight to see.
They wore blue coats
and big, wide hats.
Their shoes
had heavy wood bottoms.
Each man had
a long, black tail of hair
down his back.
They each carried
a long pole
with a bag
at the end.
Inside the bag
were clothes, food,
and a mat.
Each night
in the gold camp
they slept
on their mats.
They ate
with two sticks
instead of a fork.

The white men
laughed at the Chinese men.
"You look like clowns
with yellow skin!"
they called out.

Soo and Ping
did not understand
every word of this.
But they knew
the men were making
fun of them.

"Don't listen to them,"
said Soo.
"We will all get rich
from the gold!"

"This is too good
to be true!"
said Ping.
"I cannot believe
we are finding real gold!"

"I told you so,
little brother!"

said Soo.
"Soon the whole family
can come to California."

"No, no!"
said Ping.
"I want
to go back to China."

"We'll see
what happens,"
said Soo.
"Maybe we'll
strike it big!
But for now,
we must live
in this country.
And the sooner
we learn English,
the better off
we will be."

"You are right,"
said Ping.
"Each day we must learn
some new English words."

Not long after that,
Ping made a big strike.
It was late in the day.
"Look here!"
he called to Soo.
"Have you ever seen
such a large piece of gold?"

Soo picked up the gold.
It was
as big as an orange.
There was much more gold
where that came from.

In no time,
the whole camp
heard about the strike.
Everyone came over
to see the gold.

"That's a pretty big strike,"
said the head man.

"You get half,
we get half,"
said Soo.

"Not on a strike that big!"
laughed the head man.
"Now, you and your brother,
get out of here!
Leave this camp—
now!"

"There is no use
in fighting,"
said Ping.
"We must leave."

Soo was angry.
He felt
that fair was fair.
Why shouldn't Ping
get half the gold?

The sun
was setting
over the mountain.
Soo and Ping
tied their bags
to their poles.
In the still of the night
the two were gone.

Thinking It Over

1. If you had found
   the big piece of gold,
   what would you have done?

2. Do you think
   a deal is a deal?

3. If you were Soo and Ping,
   what would you do now?

CHAPTER 3

That night,
Soo and Ping
walked for three hours.
Then they
laid out their mats
for the night.

The next day
they walked again.
Before long,
they came upon
another gold camp.
The head man
let them join
the camp.

Most of the white men
liked working
with a pick and shovel.
Soo and Ping

liked working
in the stream.
They stood in water
all day long.
Their feet
got very cold.
Over their heads
the sun got very hot.
Soo and Ping
didn't seem to mind.

The work
was very slow.
They panned for hours
till they found gold.

"We will never hit
a big strike here,"
said Soo.

"That's OK with me,"
said Ping.
"Here we are safe.
With no big strike,
the head man
will not drive us out."

But as time went on,
they found
less and less gold.
One morning
the head man
talked to the group.

"The gold
is getting thin,"
he said.
"There is not enough work
for everyone now.
So you Chinamen
must leave the camp."

Once again
Soo was angry.
"First they drive us out
for finding too much gold,"
he said.
"Now they drive us out
for not finding enough!"

But there was nothing
they could do.

The head man
would not let them stay.
Soo and Ping
packed their things.

"Let's head north,"
said Soo.
"We'll find gold.
We'll pick over places
the white men left.
We'll find gold
on our own!"

That is
what they did.
They did not
strike it rich.
All they found
was gold dust.
For twelve years
that gold dust
kept them going.
But then
even gold dust
was hard to find.

"I really want
to go back to China,"
said Ping one day.

"We can't go home,"
said Soo.
"Not now.
We do not have
enough money.
And we could never save
enough gold dust
to pay our way home.

"Listen,"
Soo went on.
"I heard
they are starting
to build a railroad.
They need workers.
I'm tired of
trying to find gold.
There is no more gold.
I'd like to go
and build the railroad."

Thinking It Over

1. What would you do now—
   look for gold,
   build the railroad,
   or what?

2. How can you tell
   when a person
   is not afraid
   of hard work?

CHAPTER 4

"Come with me
to build the railroad."
Soo said to Ping.

"I still want
to look for gold,"
Ping answered.
"I feel
I may get lucky
one of these days."

"I'm finished with gold,"
said Soo.
"You must go your way
and I must go mine."
Soo was sad
that his brother
would not come with him.

"Sometime
we will meet again,"

said Ping.
"Good luck, my brother."

With that,
Soo and Ping Lee
parted their ways.

Soo went
to work
on the new railroad.
He joined a crew
of 10,000 men.
The white men
were paid
$35 a month.
They also got
free food.
The Chinese men
were paid
$25 a month.
And they had to
pay for their food.

Laying railroad track
was very hard.
The Chinese men

started to work
as soon as there was light.
They did not stop
until it was dark.

    Day by day
they worked their way
toward the high mountains.
At Donner Pass,
the work
became very bad.
The mountain
was covered with snow.
It snowed every day.

    The men
lived and worked under
40 feet of snow.
They cut out holes
to get air.
Every morning
they cut
a road in the snow
to get to the workplace.
Many died
that terrible winter.

And the work
became still worse
later that year.
At the top of a mountain
Soo was put
into a basket.
The basket was sent down
on a rope
along the side
of the mountain.
From inside the basket
Soo drilled holes
into the solid rock.
He put gunpowder
into the holes.
He lit the powder.
Then he pulled himself up
as fast as he could.
He got out of the way
before the rock blew up.

One night
the Chinese men
were talking.
The white men
could not understand them.

"This is not fair,"
said Lu Chin.
"We work very hard.
We do the worst work.
We work more hours.
Why don't *we*
get $35 a month?
Why don't *we*
get free food?"

"Because we are Chinese,"
said another man.

"Let's change this!"
said Soo Lee.
"Let's go on strike!
We will stop working.
We will ask
for $40 a month
and food.
We will ask
for shorter work days.
They will give us
what we want
soon enough!"

The next morning
the Chinese workers
stayed in their camp.
They did not
come out to work.
"Eight hours a day
is good for white men.
And the same thing
is good for Chinese men,"
Soo told the head man.

But the head man
did not worry
about the strike.
He used his power
against the Chinese workers.
He did not allow them
to buy any food.
There was no other way
for them to eat.
The strike
was over
the next day.

Thinking It Over

1. Do you believe
   that a work strike
   is a good way
   to win a point?

2. What is needed
   to make a strike work?

CHAPTER 5

Ping had gone north
to Oregon.
There were new gold fields
up there.
For over a year,
he panned the streams
to find more gold.
He picked over places
the white men
had left behind.

Ping worked hard.
But his luck
did not get better.
He did not find
very much gold.
"I'm starting to think
that Soo was right.
Maybe I should have
gone with him

to build the railroad,"
Ping said to himself.

Ping knew that
he had to find
a better way
to make money.
Then one day
he had an idea.

Ping had worked
in many parts of
California and Oregon.
In all those places,
he noticed
that there were
very few women around.
He knew that
most men came west
to make money.
The women
did not come along.
These men
were used to women
washing their clothes.
Here in the west

there was no one
to do it.
Washing clothes
was "women's work,"
the men said.

Some men
sent their dirty clothes
to China or Hawaii.
Once they were clean,
they were mailed back.
It cost eight dollars
to wash 12 shirts.
This was a lot of money
back then.

Ping Lee also said
that washing clothes
was women's work.
But maybe there was money
in washing clothes.

So Ping decided to
start a washhouse.
He went to San Francisco
and set up shop there.

He needed only
a few things
to get started.
He bought
some soap and a brush.
He bought
an iron and ironing board.

Ping's new washhouse
was not big and pretty.
But no one else
ever saw his workplace.
After all,
he picked up
the work.
He dropped it off
when it was finished.
Why pay rent
for a nice shop?
One room on Grant Street
would do fine.

Ping had been good
at finding gold.
Now he became good
at running a washhouse.

He turned washing clothes
into an art.

First he washed
the clothes in big tubs.
Then he hung them up
to dry.
Next he put them
into big baskets
all over the room.
He kept a water bowl
next to the ironing board.
He put his head
into the bowl.
He filled his mouth
with water.
As he shook his head,
he blew the water
over a shirt.
He checked
that the shirt
was wet enough.
He lifted
the heavy iron
from a metal box.
Under the box was a fire.

That way,
Ping didn't have to run
to the stove so often
to heat the iron.
He spit on the iron
to see if it was hot.
Then, very fast,
he ironed the shirt.
He added up the bill
on rows of beads
on the wall.
He worked
until 10:00 every night.

Ping made money
from his business
right away.
There was a need
and he filled it.
But every day,
his brother Soo
was on Ping's mind.
Where could Soo be?
Was he all right?
Would they ever
see each other again?

Thinking It Over

1. Have you ever wanted
   to start your own business?
   What would you need
   to get started?

2. Think of a job
   you have seen someone do.
   How did that person do it?

3. Do you think
   Ping and Soo
   will see each other again?

CHAPTER 6

Ping joined
the Chinese Six Companies.
This was a group
made up of many families.
It was named
for six places in China.
The members
helped Chinese people
in California.
When new Chinese people
came to town,
they welcomed them.
They helped them
find jobs.

These days,
Ping could not think
about going back home.
However,
he could not become

an American citizen
because he was Chinese.
He could not vote, either.
He just ran his business
the best he could.

But in the next few years,
his work paid off.
The gold dust
and dirty wash
brought family members
to California.
His uncle's son, Chen,
came first.

"The last time
I saw you,
you were a tiny boy,"
Ping told the young man.
"Welcome to California!"

Ping made room
for Chen
in the room
he lived in.
The Chinese Six Companies

found Chen a job
in a cigar factory.

More family members
came after that.
Ping made room
for all of them.
He made bunk beds
by nailing boards
along the walls.
He made sure
everyone had a board
to sleep on.

Other Chinese people
in San Francisco
did the same.
Grant Street
became the heart
of Chinatown.
Little by little,
Chinatown grew
into a little city
inside a big city.
Shops sold
ducks, rice, tea, and beans.

There were more Chinese people
than Ping could ever know.

Still,
there was no word
from Soo.
"A lot of Chinese died
building the railroad,"
Ping told the family.
"Soo must have been
one of them."

But far from California,
in Utah,
Soo Lee was working.
It was 1869.
The big railroad
was almost finished.
Workers from the east
met workers from the west.
At that point,
the railroad reached
from ocean to ocean.

"Be gone now,
you Chinamen!"

shouted the head man.
"Your work is done!"

All of a sudden,
Soo Lee
was out of work.
He had no place
to go.

There was a big party
where the railroad
came together.
The people
drove a gold spike
into the track.
Most of the railroad
in the west
had been built
by Chinese workers.
But the Chinese
were sent away
before the party.
It was white men only
who showed the railroad
to the world.

Thinking It Over

1. How many people
   could live in your home?

2. How important
   is your family to you?

3. Do you think
   it was fair
   to send
   the Chinese workers away?
   Would there have been
   a better time?

CHAPTER 7

Soo Lee
headed for San Francisco.
There was work there.
White workers
from the shoe factories
were on strike.
Chinese workers
were filling the jobs.

Soo wondered
about his brother.
He did not know
that Ping
was in San Francisco.

Many, many Chinese workers
came to San Francisco.
Most of them
lived in Chinatown.
Some white people
grew to hate them.

They believed
that Chinese people
were taking their jobs.

  Soo got a job
in a shoe factory.
He didn't like it.
The pay was low.
And Soo
had always worked outside.
He was not happy
at all.

  At night
Soo played cards.
Some nights
he won money.
Most nights
he lost money.
He had nothing else
to do.

  Then one night
another Chinese man
talked to Soo.
"Why don't you

join our tong?"
he said.
"Our group
will soon run
all the card games
in town.
What do you say?"

"Sure, I'll join,"
said Soo.
"I need something
to do.
I've never been afraid
to play my luck."

Soo visited card games
all over town.
He checked
on how things were run.
He took
a cut of the money.
He gave part of it
to the tong.
He kept part of it
for himself.

Before long,
all the Chinese people
were told to leave
the shoe factory.
Soo began to work full time
with the tong.

"Trouble is growing
in Chinatown,"
the tong leader
told Soo.
"White people
are coming here.
They are hurting
Chinese people.
They beat them up.
They rob them
on the street.
This must stop.
I want you
to think of ways
to help our people."

That night
Ping Lee

closed his washhouse
just like always.
He put out the fire.
He locked the doors.
He knew
about the trouble
in Chinatown.
He walked home
by himself
down Grant Street.

Thinking It Over

1. Do you think
   Ping and Soo
   will meet up?

2. What do you think
   of Soo's work
   for the tong?

3. Why would one group
   ever want to hurt
   another group?

CHAPTER 8

Ping walked
only half a block.
Then, out of the side street
jumped a group
of young white men.
Ping felt a gun
pushing on his back.

"Hand over
your money!"
they shouted.
"You have no right
to make money
in our country."

"I do not take jobs
away from you,"
said Ping.
"I only wash clothes.
No one but Chinese
wants to wash clothes."

The young men
did not listen
to what Ping
had to say.
"Give us your money
or we will kill you,"
one of them said.

"Take my money,"
Ping said.
"But I beg you
not to hurt me.
I have a big family
to take care of."

The young men
took Ping's money.
Then they hit him
over the head.
He fell
to the street.
The young men
left him for dead.

Next, the group
ran to Ping's washhouse.

They broke down
the door.
They went inside.
They smashed
everything in sight.
They threw
clothes and irons.
They laughed
the whole time.

Word came
to Soo's tong
the next day.
A washhouse
on Grant Street
had been smashed.
The owner
was robbed
in the street.
He was hurt,
but not dead.

"I want to go
to the washhouse,"
Soo told the head of the tong.
"I want to tell

the owner of the washhouse
that we can help.
He can pay us
every month.
We will make sure
he is never hurt again."

That day
Ping Lee
went to his washhouse.
He looked over
what the young men
had done.

Just then
Ping looked out
to the street.
He saw a man
walking toward the washhouse.
He knew the face
right away.
It was no longer
a young face.
But it was Soo,
all right.
It was his brother Soo.

Thinking It Over

1. Why do people like Ping get hurt sometimes?

2. What is the real purpose of the tong?

3. Is a brother or sister always a brother or sister, no matter what?

CHAPTER 9

Ping reached out
his arms.
"My brother!"
he cried.
"My long lost brother!"

"It is good
to see you!"
said Soo.
"How many years
has it been?
I should have guessed
you were in Chinatown!"

"Yes,"
said Ping.
"And I have brought over
more of our family, too!
But what brings you here?
Was it just by chance

that you were
walking down the street?"

"No. My tong
wants to help you,"
said Soo.
"We know
the white men
smashed your washhouse.
The tong
wants you to pay us
to keep trouble away.
But you are my brother.
I cannot
take your money.
I will see to it
that you are not hurt."

"I want no part
of the tong!"
said Ping.
"I run
an honest business.
The tongs
run the bad businesses.
These groups

hold no interest
to me.
But I should not be surprised
that you are in a tong.
You were always the one
to play your luck!
For me,
I am happy
to be part
of the family group."

"The family groups
are too slow to act,"
said Soo.
"They hold
too much power
in Chinatown.
You wait,
my brother.
The tongs
will rule Chinatown
in the end."

Just then
Chen walked
into the washhouse.

"Ah, Chen!"
said Ping.
"Meet your cousin.
This is my brother, Soo."

Soo and Chen
shook hands.

"I am glad
to meet my blood,"
said Soo.
"If you ever need help,
let me know."

"Thank you,"
said Chen.

"Where are you going?"
Ping asked Chen.

"To the dance hall,"
said the young man.

"Why do you go there?"
Ping wanted to know.

"I am meeting
a woman there,"
said Chen.

"They are not good women,"
said Ping.
"There are
only singsong girls
at the dance hall.
You cannot trust them.
You should keep away
from those women."

"But they are
the only Chinese women
in town!"
laughed Soo.
"Let the boy go
and have a good time."

"Very well,"
said Ping.
"Soo is my older brother.
If he says you may go,
then go."

"Maybe I
will see you sometime
at the dance hall,"
said Soo to Chen.
"Now, Ping,
let's talk
about your washhouse.
I will make sure
you are safe."

"No strings?"
Ping asked.

"No strings,"
said Soo.
"We are family.
Blood must come first."

Thinking It Over

1. Do you believe
    that "blood must come first"?

2. Would you be a member
    of a tong or a family group?
    Why?

3. Would you let the young man
    go to the dance hall?

4. What is the meaning
    of "no strings"?

CHAPTER **10**

Not long after that,
Soo went
to the dance hall.

"Hey, Soo!"
called one of his tong friends.
"Look over there!
Another man
is with your girl!"

Soo saw the girl
he liked best
on the other side
of the room.
She was beautiful.
Soo loved
her long, black hair.
She always wore
a flower in it.
Everyone called her
the Flower Girl.

The tong
had brought the Flower Girl
from China.
She and the other girls
worked in the dance hall.
The Flower Girl
was very young.
Soo was almost 40.
He watched the girl
as she talked
with the young man.

Soo started
to walk up to her.
Then he stopped
in his tracks.
The Flower Girl
was talking with Chen!

"Do you want
some help?"
the tong friend asked Soo.
"Do you want us
to send
her little friend home?"

Soo was ready
to say no.
But it was too late.
His tong friends headed
toward the Flower Girl's table.
They pulled Chen
off his chair.
They pushed him
toward the front door.

"Keep your hands
off the Flower Girl!"
the tong members
told Chen.

Just then,
another man stood up.
"What do you think
you are doing?"
shouted the man.
"That young man
is a Lee.
And so are we.
Get your hands
off him!"

In a second,
the tong men
and members of the family group
were fighting.
Tables and chairs
flew all over the room.

The fight
spilled into the street.
Before long,
the fight
had become a small war.
There was blood and glass
all over the street.

Young Chen Lee
headed home.
He was not hurt.
But he was afraid
to face Uncle Ping.

Thinking It Over

1. What would you think
   of this fight
   if you were Ping?

2. Have you ever
   seen a fight break out?
   How did it start?

CHAPTER 11

"You are
my older brother,"
Ping said to Soo.
"But I
must tell you this.
Blood should not
fight blood!
I hate these wars!
You cannot be
a Lee and belong
to a tong.
You are
first a Lee."

"The fight
over the Flower Girl
was not my idea,"
said Soo.
"But I am not part
of the family group, either.
I believe

in the tong.
If the tong
can help you,
then fine.
If not,
then I am sorry."

"There is a way
you can stop the fight
over the Flower Girl,"
said Ping.
"Get Chen
a wife.
Bring over
a good woman
from China."

"I will do
the best I can,"
said Soo.
"It won't be easy.
The Americans
are trying to stop
any more Chinese people
from coming here.
We will have to work fast."

Soo and the tong
were used to working fast.
But this time
they could not work
fast enough.
A new law
was passed.
The law said that
no new Chinese workers
could come to America.
Women and children
could not come
if their men
worked in factories or farms.
Only business owners
could bring their families
over from China.

"There is only one way
to bring a woman
for Chen,"
Soo told Ping.
"Chen must stop working
in the factory.
He must run
his own business.

Then we must say
that he was married
in China."

    Ping did not like
to lie.
But he had an idea.
"Chen,"
he began.
"I am getting old.
I will give you
my washhouse.
You may run it
as your own.
I can work
for you."

    So Chen
took over the washhouse.
Soo made papers
saying Chen was married
in China.

    In a few months
Chen had a wife.

Her name was Kam.
At last,
the Lees
had a woman
in the house.
And, for now,
there was peace
in the family.

Thinking It Over

1. Do you think that
   the Lees broke the law
   to bring the woman
   from China?

2. Do you think
   the law against Chinese people
   was fair?

CHAPTER 12

The street wars
between the families
and the tongs
went on for many years.
Soo's power
in the tong grew.
Ping's power
in the family group grew.
The tongs and the families
both wanted power
over Chinatown.

Many times,
Ping's family group
and Soo's tong
fought each other.
After one such war,
Ping went to see Soo.

"Blood must not fight blood,"
Ping told Soo.

"I have said this before.
We cannot let this be.
You and I
are brothers.
We can be the bridge
between the groups.
I want you
to sit
with our group.
Let us work together
for power and peace
in Chinatown."

"Yes,"
said Soo.
"Let us work together.
We are too old
to fight
in the street.
But we are not too old
to talk."

The groups
began to work together
instead of against each other.
With the help

of the Lee brothers,
peace began to come.

By 1906,
Soo and Ping Lee
were old men.
One morning,
very early,
they were both
sleeping in their beds.
All of a sudden,
Soo felt drops of water
on his head.
He woke up
right away.
Just then, everything
began to shake.

It was an earthquake!
It had cracked
the water pipe.
Water came down
all over Soo's room.

He got out of bed
as fast as he could.

He pulled on
his clothes.
The first thing he did
was to go
to the washhouse.

   Ping and Chen
were standing outside.
The washhouse
was on fire.
Soon much of the city
was on fire.
Many of the buildings
were falling down.

   The earthquake
was terrible.
But in one way
it helped the Chinese
in San Francisco.
Important papers
were lost.
Now no one knew for sure
which Chinese were born
in America.

"Now I can bring over
my son from China!"
said Soo.

"What do you mean?"
asked Ping.
"You do not have
a son!"

"I can have
a 'paper son'!"
said Soo.
"Without real papers,
I can say
I had a son
in China.
No one will ever know
if it's true or not!"

"You always have
come up with
bright ideas!"
said Ping.
"You will never stop,
will you?"

Before he died,
Soo brought over
three young men.
It made him happy.

Ping was glad to have
Chen's family.
Chen and Kam
had five children.
Ping was like a grandfather
to them.

Peace came
for the Chinese in America.
But it happened
only after Soo and Ping
were gone.
The tong wars ended.
But not until 1944
could the Chinese
become American citizens.
Chen's children
were among the first.

Chen's children
never forgot

the story
of Soo and Ping.
They knew
that peace had come
at a high cost.
It took the gold rush.
It took the railroad.
It took the washhouse.
It took the tong wars.
It took the earthquake.
It took family blood.
It took many hard years
to bring the Chinese in America
a better life.

Thinking It Over

1. Why do you think
   life was not fair
   for the Chinese in America?

2. Why do you think
   there was so much fighting
   in Chinatown?

3. What does it take
   to make life
   as fair as possible?